Songbirds
of the Eastern and Central States

Paintings by
Kathryn DeVos-Miller

Text by
Trudy L. Rising

Tundra Books

First printing.

Tundra Books of Northern New York
Plattsburgh, New York 12901
ISBN 0-912766-58-1
12 prepack ISBN 0-912766-72-7
Library of Congress Card No. 77-070451

Printed in the United States

Preface

The birds we have selected are among the most common songbirds representing each of the families found in the eastern half of North America (in the west, many of these birds are replaced by other species).

Kathryn DeVos-Miller used museum specimens, slides and photographs of the birds as aids in selecting poses and determining proper body structure for her illustrations.

Probably many readers will be surprised to see birds like the crow or blue jay included in a book about songbirds. To qualify, a bird need not be a gifted singer. What the birds must have is a number of characteristics in common that show they are related to one another, in the Order Passeriformes ("songbirds"). Although ornithologists recognize many such orders, about 3/5 of the more than 8600 kinds of birds in the world are classified as songbirds. All of these 5000 or so species have more than four pairs of muscles (syrinx muscles) controlling voice production; feet adapted for perching, with four unwebbed toes joined at the same level; and have young that are hatched naked and helpless, requiring parental care. These are the most obvious similarities.

The songbirds are listed here in a standard order. For example, the nuthatches and chickadees are very similar birds and, thus, are grouped together. Similarly the sparrows, buntings, finches, warblers, tanagers and blackbirds form a large group of closely related birds. As more fossil evidence is accumulated and more physical and chemical studies of the birds are done, relationships will become clearer.

When reading this book about birds (or other books about the lives of other animals), try not to impose human standards on these animals. For example, males of some species do not help incubate the eggs or care for the young. But we cannot say that the male is a poor parent. His behavior simply adapts to his environment.

In North America, the number of people who can identify the many kinds of birds is ever increasing. However, knowing something about these birds is another matter. Though excellent field guides are available for identification (Roger Tory Peterson's **A Field Guide to the Birds,** Robin's and Bruun's **Birds of North America**), there are few books that tell how the birds live. Those that exist are great volumes that are usually costly. In this small book, I have tried to condense what is known about some of these winged, feathered creatures using as little technical jargon as possible. We hope you'll want to go look for some of them after you've read the book.

Although the information about each species is derived from a variety of sources, A. C. Bent's classic volumes on the **Life Histories of North American Birds,** 1919-58, United States National Museum, were especially rich sources of material. The songbirds are listed according to the order found in **Avian Biology,** edited by Donald S. Farner and James R. King, Academic Press, 1971.

Trudy L. Rising

To Jim Rising whose love and knowledge
of these animals made our doing a book
about them possible.

Contents

1 Eastern Kingbird
Tyrannus tyrannus
Le Tyran tritri

Although smaller than a robin, the king-bird does not hesitate to attack crows, vultures, even hawks. The unsuspecting bird, small or large, is suddenly met by a kingbird diving out at it with a harsh scream. Sometimes the kingbird lands on the back of the bird it is chasing and pecks at it as it tries to fly away. Kingbirds have been known to go after birdwatchers who come too close with their cameras. One was even seen chasing a low-flying airplane!

No wonder that Indians called this bird "little chief" and that its Latin name is **Tyrannus tyrannus.**

The kingbird has also been called "bee martin" or "bee bird" because of its habit of seeking out honeybee hives. For this reason it was considered a pest and shot. But now, like all songbirds, it is protected by law.

A member of the flycatcher family, the kingbird sits upright on its perch, quiet and alert, waiting for an insect to fly past. When one does, the bird lunges forward, snaps at its prey with a quick click of the bill, then returns to its perch to wait for another insect. You'll rarely see a fly-catcher walk or hop. Weak-footed, it always flies from perch to perch.

The mating song of the kingbird is a simple shrill cry. The courtship that follows is often dramatic, with the male swooping and diving near a female. Male and female look alike: plain-colored except for the reddish-orange crown on their heads which is visible only when they are alarmed. Their noisy, aggressive habits make them one of the most commonly seen birds of open country.

7.8-8.7", 20-22 cm; 3-5 eggs, creamy white with brownish splotches; rough nest of twigs and stalks, lined with fine grasses, in trees in orchards; winters South America.

2 Horned Lark

Eremophila alpestris
L'Alouette cornue

During mating season the male Horned Lark
puts on quite a show. He flies straight up,
high into the air, making no sound. Then,
spreading his wings and soaring, he sings a
beautiful, joyful song. After flapping his
wings a few times, he soars again and repeats his song. Then, as suddenly and
silently as he went up, he plunges to earth,
spreading his wings just before you think
he is going to crash into the ground. He
struts around with his wings drooping and
the black-feather "horns" on his head
sticking up, partly to attract a mate and
partly to keep other males away.

Females build a simple nest on the ground,
using any handy materials. In the north
the nest may be sunk into reindeer moss
and lined with ptarmigan feathers and
caribou hair. They often lay their first
eggs before the snow has melted.

When the eggs hatch, both male and female
are very active in feeding their young. One
birdwatcher noted that a pair of Horned
Larks fed their nestlings 108 times in one
day. (Baby birds of most species have to
be fed so frequently that they rarely survive when people try to look after them.)

Look for Horned Larks walking, not
hopping, along the ground in any open
place — prairies, airports, shores, Arctic
tundra, cultivated fields. You'll have to
look closely because their dull brown color
camouflages them well. This is the only
lark native to North America. The meadowlark, in spite of its name, is not a lark but
a kind of blackbird.

6.8-8", 17-20 cm; 3-5 eggs, grayish, speckled
with pale brown; winters southern Canada to
Gulf of Mexico.

3 Tree Swallow

Iridoprocne bicolor
L'Hirondelle bicolore

You might be able to get a family of Tree Swallows to nest in your backyard by putting out wooden nest boxes, as these birds are easily attracted to birdhouses. (Make the entrance less than 1-1/2'' or 3.8 cm in diameter if you want to keep starlings out.) Tree Swallows also build nests in old woodpecker holes and dead trees in flooded areas. A colony of Tree Swallows nested in the midst of great activity near the train station at the amusement park on Centre Island in Toronto one year. (The site was used by House Sparrows and Purple Martins the next year.) These little birds have even been known to build nests in a moving boat!

In August, swallows begin to form loose flocks to fly south. You might see hundreds or even thousands in flight. As evening approaches, watch for them along roadsides. Huge numbers often line up on fences and wires. The Tree Swallow is distinguished from other swallows by its white underparts. It is the last swallow to leave in fall and the first to return in spring.

Tree Swallows eat some berries and seeds but mainly insects caught in flight over meadows and ponds. Of greatest danger to these birds is prolonged cold or rainy weather which forces insects into shelter. Unable to obtain enough food, young or weak birds cannot survive.

Watch for these magnificent flyers, the swallows, who spend more time in the air than any other passerine (perching) birds.

5-6.2'', 13-16 cm; 4-6 eggs, white; simple nest dry grass and straw, feather lining; winters from North Carolina to Honduras and Cuba.

4 Barn Swallow
Hirundo rustica
L'Hirondelle des granges

The Barn Swallow is among the most
domestic of wild animals, often found
associated with people and showing little
fear of them. Though sometimes they
build their nests in cliff holes or on rocky
ledges, more often they will choose a man-
made place: eaves of buildings, undersides
of bridges and of course the rough beams
of old-fashioned North American barns.
Farmers welcome these birds as eaters of
insects.

Once the site is selected, the birds work
hard at building their nest. One birdwatcher
saw a pair of Barn Swallows work fourteen
hours a day for eight days on their nest,
bringing a load of straw, grass or pellets of
mud every two to three minutes.

Fortunately, the days when Barn Swallow
feathers were used for women's hats are
long gone. Massive slaughter of these animals in the 1800's was stopped as a result
of publicity by naturalists. The Audubon
Society was formed shortly after, in part
as a response to this destruction of bird
life.

The Barn Swallow is the most widespread
songbird in the world, easily distinguished
from other North American swallows by
its long, deeply forked tail. Like all
swallows, they spend most of their time in
flight catching insects in their gaping beaks
as they fly.

Everyone welcomes this friendly bird and
loves to hear its light, bubbling, trilling song.

5.8-7.7", 15-20 cm; 4-6 eggs, white with brownish spots; winters Mexico to Brazil.

5 Loggerhead (Migrant) Shrike
Lanius ludovicianus
La Pie-grièche migratrice

A small mouse or grasshopper impaled on barbed wire is an unpleasant sight — it is also the sign of a shrike. Like many other predators, shrikes often kill more than they can eat and leave a number of creatures impaled at one time. (The habit of impaling probably developed because of the difficulty shrikes have holding tough-hided animals with their feet while tearing them apart with their beaks.) Shrikes are sometimes called "butcher birds" and — not surprisingly — are among the least loved of the songbirds.

Shrikes have poor songs — their name *Lanius* comes from the same root as "shriek." They live more a hawk's life than a songbird's. Shrikes are usually seen alone, perched at the top of a tree, telephone pole or fence post, sitting straight up — hawklike — watching quietly for prey. Unlike hawks, they capture and kill with their hooked beaks rather than with their talons. Their feet, though strong, are not well-adapted to killing. Like hawks and owls, shrikes regurgitate the indigestible bones and fur of their prey.

In courtship the male shrike flutters his wings and spreads his tail in display, but if he displays for too long, the female chases him away. At the nest, the male stands guard and brings food to the female while she incubates the eggs. Often he is still feeding the young of the first nest while the female is laying the second batch of eggs.

Shrikes are not highly migratory, moving only far enough to find a good food supply.

8.6-9.2", 22-23 cm; 4-6 eggs, grayish white, spotted with gray and brown; bulky nest of woven sticks, twigs, weeds, lined with soft materials, in dense foliage of trees; winters north-central U.S. through Mexico.

6 Cedar Waxwing
Bombycilla cedrorum
Le Jaseur des cèdres

Cedar Waxwings — so named because of waxlike droplets hanging from their wings — are friendly, gregarious birds. They are often seen sitting side by side, a half dozen or so, passing berries up and down the line.

Their love of cherries gave them another name: "cherry bird." Early in this century, Vermont fruit growers pushed to make it legal to shoot waxwings. It is said that state senators voted against the action after seeing the bird: they thought it too beautiful to kill.

Cedar Waxwings also eat wild fruit and insects, and are called "cankerbirds" because they eat many destructive caterpillars, or cankerworms.

When the blue berries of cedars are ripe, waxwings gorge themselves to such an extent that they are sometimes unable to fly afterwards. One birdwatcher reported seeing a flock of Cedar Waxwings tumbling around and bobbing in such an unnatural way that he concluded that fermented juices from overripe berries had made them drunk. (Robins have also been seen in this condition.)

Waxwings are so friendly all year round it's hard to tell when courtship begins. It seems to begin when one bird acts as if it wishes to be fed. Its wings tremble and whirl and it emits rattlelike sounds. It rushes to another bird against whom it rubs its breast, and then returns to its perch. The other bird reciprocates, and they often offer petals to each other.

6.5-8", 17-20 cm; 3-5 eggs, pale bluish gray or greenish blue, spots or dots of black or dark brown; loosely woven nest, grass, twigs, soft lining; in open woods, orchards; winters in southern Canada through eastern and central U.S.

7 Winter Wren
Troglodytes troglodytes
Le Troglodyte des forêts

This is the same wren that is known in England as the "Jenny Wren"; its German name means "king of the hedges." Wherever it is found, the Winter Wren has for centuries been a popular bird.

For a small bird, the Winter Wren sings an amazing song. Full and rich, it lasts only six to nine seconds but contains 106-113 separate notes!

Winter Wrens usually build their nests in the upturned roots of fallen trees. The male will, in fact, build several large bulky nests of moss, grass and roots. The female chooses the best constructed and concealed of these, lines it with hair and feathers and builds a roof over it, leaving a small round entrance hole. While the female incubates the eggs in this nest, the male sleeps in one of the other "dummy" nests.

Many Winter Wrens move south in the winter, but they are back on their breeding grounds in April — often while snow is still on the ground.

Because they are small and live close to the ground in tangled underbrush, they are sometimes hard to find. Listen for their melodious songs and their harsh scolding calls, and watch for an active, insect-eating bird with a stubby, cocked tail that bobs up and down.

4-4.5", 10-11 cm; 5-6 eggs, white, dotted with reddish brown; winters southern Canada to Texas and Florida.

8 Catbird
Dumetella carolinensis
Le Moqueur-chat

Though most people recognize this bird by its rattling, catlike mewing call, the Catbird also has a pleasant song which can last as long as five minutes. Though not the mimic that its relative the Mockingbird is, the Catbird is quick to pick up other birds' songs.

While the female builds her nest, the male sings, almost continuously, often late into the night. The female makes a nest of twigs, grasses and leaves so deeply cupped that when she sits on it her tail is thrust up high and her head is thrown back — an extremely uncomfortable-looking position to sit in for twelve or thirteen days!

Catbirds have a very strong feeding drive; they often feed the brood of another kind of bird, especially if their own young are lost. On the other hand, they have also been seen eating the eggs of other species.

Because their nests are usually in dense thickets near the ground, Catbirds fall prey to foxes, cats and snakes. But one black-snake met its match when it came too close to a Catbird nest — it was violently attacked by four Catbirds, two kingbirds, an oriole and a wren.

Sadly, the person who saw this happen shot the snake as it was driven away from the nest. But increasing numbers of people are realizing the importance of predators such as snakes in maintaining a balance in nature.

8.4-9.4", 21-24 cm; 3-5 eggs, glossy, deep greenish blue; winters southeast U.S., Central America.

9 American Robin
Turdus migratorius
Le Merle américain

Though the robin's song is not spectacular, it is one of the best known and most welcomed bird songs in North America. These large thrushes are early risers and some begin singing their pleasant, long-continued "cheerily, cheerily" even before daybreak.

Stop sometime to watch a robin search for earthworms. After each run across a lawn the bird stops, looks around, tilts its head from side to side, then suddenly thrusts its bill through the grass to grab a worm. Then the tug of war begins: the robin leans back, bracing its feet while the worm digs its bristles into the walls of its burrow. Usually the robin wins the battle, pulls the worm from the ground, loops it in its bill and flies off to its perch or nest. Robins also eat fruit, and in large flocks do great damage to orchards.

There are many more robins today than there were before the land was cleared. Their worst enemy is the domestic cat which is estimated to catch an average of fifty birds of various kinds in one year.

Though robins migrate, some do not go far, stopping in New England or southern Ontario for the winter. So if you see a robin in February, it isn't necessarily a sign that spring is on the way.

By the way, our American Robin is not the "Robin Redbreast" of so many old English stories. Early English settlers named the American Robin after a smaller, red-breasted bird found in their homeland — one of their favorites.

The robin is the state bird of Connecticut, Michigan and Wisconsin.

9-10.8", 23-27 cm; 4 eggs, plain blue; deeply cupped nest, grasses, weeds, cloth, molded with mud, lined with fine grasses, in shrubs, tree forks, buildings.

10 Wood Thrush

Hylocichla mustelina
La Grive des bois

In low, cool, damp forests, the Wood Thrush sings its flutelike "ee-o-lay" as soon as it arrives in spring. Males sing their most elaborate and vigorous songs early in the season.

The Wood Thrush has one of the most beautiful songs among songbirds. Once you've heard it, you won't be surprised to learn that it is a close relative of that well-known singer, the European Nightingale. Only the males of most songbirds sing elaborate songs, but the female Wood Thrush sings beautifully, too — even while incubating her eggs!

After mating, the female chooses a site in the fork of a tree and begins building a nest, while the male guards the territory. Wood Thrushes will tolerate other kinds of birds in the area — but violently attack other Wood Thrushes.

Watch for this plump, speckle-breasted, large-eyed bird on the forest floor where it will be searching for insects among the mushrooms and ferns.

7.5-8.5", 19-22 cm; 3-4 eggs, pale blue or bluish green; nest of grasses, weeds, trash, molded with mud or leaf mold; winters Central America.

11 Eastern Bluebird
Sialia sialis
Le Merle bleu à poitrine rouge

This beautiful blue bird with the soft, gurgly voice was once common in North America. But House Sparrows and starlings, brought from Britain, took many of the nesting cavities that had been used by bluebirds and their number began to decline. Now bluebirds can be found only where plenty of birdhouses are available for them to nest in. If you want to attract bluebirds, build a birdhouse on a pole, 5-10 feet or 1.5-3.1 meters high, in the open, with an entrance of 1-1/2 inches or 3.8 cm (to keep starlings out). House Wrens and Tree Swallows also use this size entrance but bluebirds can hold their own in competition with them.

Bluebirds have a beautiful courtship. Fluttering with widespread tail and half-open wings, and singing a soft song, the male perches beside the female, caresses her and brings her food. He often leads her to a cavity or nest box and looks in. The female chooses the nesting site, however, and it isn't always the one the male showed her.

Bluebirds are not loyal to their mates and often choose another for the second brood, and still another for the third.

When it's time for nestlings to be fledged, the parents leave the nest and, from a distance, sing for them to come out. When one finally comes tumbling out — probably from hunger — both parents rush down to feed it.

Bluebirds hop along the ground or dart among the foliage of trees looking for insects; they also catch insects while in flight. And they sometimes eat fruit, mostly wild.

6.5-7.7", 17-20 cm; 3-6 eggs, glossy, pale blue or bluish white; loosely built cup of fine grasses, weed stalks, leaves in cavities; winters north-central U.S. through Mexico.

12 Golden-crowned Kinglet

Regulus satrapa
Le Roitelet à couronne dorée

Ruby-crowned Kinglet

Regulus calendula
Le Roitelet à couronne rubis

Regulus, the Kinglet's Latin name, means "little king," and these birds do put on regal airs during mating season. The males flash their bright crowns at each other, spread their tails, and fluff out their side feathers. They don't fight, but they do follow each other emitting high shrill calls all the while.

The Ruby-crowned Kinglet goes farther north in summer and farther south in winter than the Golden-crowned. Its migration is also more conspicuous because unlike most birds it sings in migration. You'll see — and hear — it in thickets, trees and shrubbery around houses in April.

The tiny, stubby, active kinglets flit about constantly searching for insects. They look through clusters of pine needles, peering about the base of each needle and in pockets between needles. Sometimes they hover before the clusters, looking for insects. They catch an insect of some kind — usually a wasp or ant — every five or six seconds. When insects are not available, they eat small seeds.

Ruby-crowned Kinglets have a pleasant warbling song that is quite melodious and fairly loud — you'd expect it to come from a much bigger bird. The Golden-crowned Kinglet's song is so high-pitched that it is difficult for the human ear to detect.

3.4-4.5", 9-11 cm (ruby); 3.5-4", 9-10 cm (golden); 5-11 eggs, pale white, fine reddish-brown dots; deeply cupped hanging nest, well concealed in conifer, usually spruce; nest of mosses, lichens, twigs bound by fibers from insect cocoons; winters southern Canada to Central America.

13 Brown Creeper

Certhia familiaris
Le Grimpereau brun

Most people associate birds with flight and freedom. The Brown Creeper flies little, and some people feel sorry for it because of the "boring" life it leads. I personally find it fascinating to watch.

The Brown Creeper spends all day, every day, climbing trees. It starts at the bottom and — using its stiff tail as a prop — it climbs, making a spiral motion around the tree all the way to the top. It then flutters to the base of the next tree and repeats the pattern. One observer watched as a Brown Creeper climbed 43 trees in one hour in its search for insects. The creeper works alone, oblivious to other small birds around it which are also searching for insects in the bark. It emits high-pitched squeaks while feeding and fluttering from tree to tree. This "zi-i-i-it" is difficult for the human ear to detect. The creeper seems to see poorly when engrossed in this activity, and occasionally mistakes a pant leg for a tree.

Creepers do fly during courtship — weaving in and out of trees, making wild dashes back and forth, sometimes chasing each other. The female creeper builds the nest, usually behind a slab of bark that is beginning to peel off. She makes a loose, hammock-shaped nest on a foundation of twigs and spider cocoons.

The Brown Creeper is an excellent example of protective coloration because its plumage closely resembles the tree it climbs. When pursued by a shrike or hawk, the creeper flattens itself against the tree, wings spread out, and remains completely still. A bird-watcher notes that even he has lost sight of creepers when they hide themselves this way.

5-5.75", 13-15 cm; 4-8 eggs, white, creamy white, spotted with reddish brown; winters in breeding range south to Texas and Florida.

14 Black-capped Chickadee
Parus atricapillus
La Mésange à tête noire

Happily for us, the small, fluffy Black-capped Chickadee is a common bird of the woodlands. Its simple, cheerful "chick-a-dee-dee" is heard year round.

Chickadees cling to branches in every imaginable position — upside down, sideways, right side up — as they search the bark for insect eggs and caterpillars. They also eat bayberries, blueberries, poison ivy berries and seeds. They hold seeds between their feet and pound them with their bills.

Snow bothers the chickadees very little. They fluff up their feathers to keep warm and carry on. Since their food supply is available year round, they don't migrate.

While courting in the spring, male chickadees whistle "fee-bee" which to some people sounds like "spring time" or "spring's here." The chickadees' nest site is usually a cavity or tree stump. It takes them about fourteen days to complete the nest: ten days excavating the cavity and carrying away the rotten wood, and four days building the nest.

These little birds seem to be quite intelligent. A U.S. government handler noticed that of the dozen or so species in his traps, only Black-capped Chickadees remembered the way out — and they did it directly, without searching for the exit.

Black-capped Chickadees are readily attracted to feeders. To entice them put out suet and sunflower seeds. They are tame enough that with patience you can get them to eat from your hand.

To learn about the White-breasted Nuthatch illustrated here, turn to a description of it following the cowbird (No. 43).

4.8-5.7", 12-15 cm; 6-8 eggs, white, small reddish-brown spots, smooth shell, little gloss.

15 Canada (Gray) Jay
Perisoreus canadensis
Le Geai gris

Have you ever felt that you were being watched and followed as you walked in northern woods? Perhaps you were — by a Canada Jay. After a silent, inquisitive introduction, the jay usually makes its presence known.

This subtly beautiful bird is so curious and shows so little fear of man that it can become a pest. Notorious for grabbing food wherever it can, it has been reported to take food right off a plate, enter tents, pry open boxes and carry off anything from soap to tobacco. These jays have huge salivary glands which aid them in pasting food in hollows of trees, their storehouses for the winter. In winter, they also raid cabins and northern settlements for food.

Because Canada Jays are large, active and noisy, it is difficult not to be aware of their presence after a short time in the dense, northern woods. Known to mimic hawks and make whistling sounds that aren't usually attributed to jays, they may deceive you if you only hear and not see them.

Canada Jays are quiet only during breeding season. And they are careful in nesting season to keep the ground below their nest clean of litter or droppings. Both are guards against predators finding their nests.

The people of the far north who know this bird best call it "whiskey Jack," which comes from its Indian name — "wiss-ka-chon." Others call it "camp robber," "moose bird," "venison hawk," and "Hudson Bay bird."

10.8-12.2", 27-31 cm; 2-6 eggs, grayish, olive spots; large, thick-walled nest in fir or spruce tree.

16 Blue Jay
Cyanocitta cristata
Le Geai bleu

Blue Jays are notorious for pestering hawks and owls. If a jay finds an owl perched in a tree, it cries to other jays, and before the poor owl knows what's happening, there's a screaming blue and white feathery mob after it. They chase the owl from tree to tree, diving at it, but rarely actually hitting it.

Though the Blue Jay has beautiful plumage, it usually calls attention to itself by all the noise it makes: calling "jay, jay," screaming, whistling, chattering and squawking. Blue Jays imitate other birds and have been heard giving the song of the Baltimore Oriole, the cry of the hawk, and the mew of the Catbird. The scream of an alarmed Blue Jay is unmistakable. Blue crest erect, it loudly calls other jays for help. Other animals seem to recognize this as a danger signal. A man reported following a porcu-

pine down a forest trail. The porcupine didn't notice him until warned of danger by the scream of a jay. Only then did the porcupine put up his quills, sniff around, and run into the woods.

The only time a Blue Jay is quiet is during mating season. If you spot a jay during this time and try to follow it back to its nest, you'll almost surely fail. The bird is very wary of danger and careful not to lead an intruder to its young.

Blue Jays eat almost anything. They do nest rob, but less than we tend to think. In winter, they are easily attracted to feeders and some migrate to regions where food is plentiful.

11-12.5", 28-32 cm; 4-6 eggs, buff or greenish, dark brown spots; bulky well-hidden nest.

17 Common Crow
Corvus brachyrhynchos
La Corneille américaine

"If men wore feathers and wings a very few of them would be clever enough to be crows." Henry Ward Beecher's famous quote says well what people have long thought of the crow's intelligence. Crows quickly learn different shapes, and they mimic other birds and human sounds including laughter. They break clam shells by flying high and dropping them to the rocks below; when a group of crows are feeding, one crow acts as sentry, warning the others when intruders approach. Whether these are signs of learning ability, or simply habits that were selected through the evolutionary process is hard to say.

My family and I came upon a crow like the one illustrated here in a perfect spot to meet such a symbol of evil. We had stopped to investigate an old wood-frame church (on a deserted road and in the rain; what could be better?). The crow flew down, cawing at us, and blocked our entrance until we fed it some tasty morsels.

In the spring, crows rattle and coo as they pair up for nesting season. They have quite a courtship ritual. The male bows, struts, and sings his rattling song to the female — sometimes again and again. Once accepted by a female, the two caress with beaks and pick gently at each other's heads. Nests are built high in a conifer or oak.

Crows are omnivores, eating almost anything. Thus, they're often disliked. Despite attempts to get rid of them by poisoning, shooting or bombing their roosts, crows have survived and are found almost every-where.

17-21", 43-53 cm; 4-6 eggs, greenish, spotted with brown; large, crude-looking nest.

18 Common Starling
Sturnus vulgaris
L'Etourneau sansonnet

In 1889 there were no starlings in North America. Now there are millions. In 1890-91, a British immigrant released about 100 starlings in New York City's Central Park. He, and others who had tried to introduce them before him, thought the birds were pleasant to have around. Today, millions of New Yorkers — and other city dwellers – disagree with him. The starling is a poor housekeeper; its nest is usually untidy and often foul-smelling. It's no wonder city dwellers dislike the starlings' habit of roosting in large numbers in buildings. Large flocks are a nuisance to farmers because of the large amount of grain they eat, although smaller numbers can be beneficial because they also eat insects.

Starlings compete with many other birds for nest sites and food. Some species have become greatly reduced in number since the starling was introduced. Sometimes they move into a newly excavated bird's hole chasing the original occupant away. They occasionally kill the other bird's young or throw out its eggs.

The starling's unpopularity is not due to its appearance, for it is a lovely bird with shiny black feathers and hues of purple and green. The flight of a flock is a beautiful sight, too, as all the birds move together in a huge black cloud. If a hawk approaches, the flock gathers tighter and chases it, always staying safely above the hawk.

Starlings squeak, chatter, rattle, chirp and wheeze. They also whistle and mimic other birds. They sing the Wood Pewee's "pee-a-wee" so often that birdwatchers used to think it was the starlings' own song.

7.5-8.5", 19-22 cm; 4-5 eggs, pale bluish or greenish white; loosely built straw and grass nest, in cavity or hole almost anywhere.

19 House Sparrow (English Sparrow)

Passer domesticus

Le Moineau domestique

This bird was introduced to North America in 1853 — fifty were released in a Brooklyn cemetery much to the regret of later generations of farmers and city dwellers. Farmers consider House Sparrows a nuisance because of the amount of grain they eat and because they spread pests like chicken mites by feeding in one barnyard after another. City dwellers dislike the birds because they are found in such large numbers in urban areas. Noisy and boisterous, they always seem to be chirping and chattering, and have been accused of driving away other species.

Nevertheless, they are interesting, adaptable, pretty little creatures. According to birdwatchers, these birds often display considerable intelligence. One observer saw a male House Sparrow bring a goose feather to his nest, lay it there and fly off. A female House Sparrow, nesting nearby, flew to his nest, took the goose feather and hid it in the fork of a nearby tree. When the male returned and found the feather missing, he immediately flew to the nest of the thief. Not finding the feather, he scolded all the birds in sight and finally flew away. Then the thief flew to the tree, recovered the feather and took it to her own nest.

During breeding, a male hops back and forth in front of a female to attract her. If she ignores him, other males peck at her tail. She doesn't always respond immediately, but she will soon after accept a male.

House Sparrows are diligent parents who never abandon their young. If one falls from the nest, father or mother feeds and shelters it on the ground until it can fly. These parents form permanent pairs, usually for life.

5.8-6.7", 15-17 cm; 3-7 eggs, white, greenish white dotted with grays, browns.

20 Evening Grosbeak
Hesperiphona vespertina
Le Gros-bec errant

The Evening Grosbeak's scientific name is from the Greek ''Hesperides'' meaning ''daughters of night.'' It was once thought that this bird sings just in the evening, but you can hear it at any time of day.

These birds were once found only in the west, but when Box Elder trees were planted further east, the birds followed — the seeds of the Box Elder are their favorite food — and now they are found throughout the eastern part of the country.

Evening Grosbeaks nest high in pines and spruces so their nests are hard to find. Unlike most songbirds, the female grosbeak does most of the singing and often displays more than the male in breeding season.

They spend the winter from southern Canada to the central states in the United States. Their body feathers cover a gray down that keeps them warm. They have short feet that can be tucked under their feathers, and the ridged, cornified cushions on the bottoms of their feet are good for gripping icy branches.

When snow is heavy, Evening Grosbeaks congregate at feeders, packing in tightly, pushing each other off and chasing away other kinds of birds. Put out sunflower seeds for them. After a while, they will become less wary of you. But be careful around them: they have beaks powerful enough to break a cherry stone.

You can recognize a migrating flock by their slight undulation in flight and by the loud ringing ''p-teer, p-teer'' they make with each dip of their bodies.

7-8.5'', 18-22 cm; 2-5 eggs, blue or blue-green blotched with shades of brown, gray, purple; oblong cupped nest, high in conifer.

21 Common Redpoll
Acanthis flammea
Le Sizerin à tête rouge

Most of us know redpolls as winter visitors.
They breed in the northern parts of Canada's
eastern provinces. At summer's end, they
fly south — rarely farther than South
Carolina and Kansas — and in winter you
may see large flocks of them feeding by
roadsides, looking for seeds. They also take
in lots of gravel, to grind the seeds.

Redpoll nestlings are most often fed
between 3 a.m. and 6 a.m. This is because
these birds spend the summer in the far
north where it's daylight by that time.

Listen for the double-noted "zit, zit"
when you see flocks of small birds
arriving about September.

4.5-6", 11-15 cm; 5-6 eggs spotted with reddish
brown; nest of grass and twigs, lined with plant
down, feathers, fur, on ground, in rock crevices.

White-winged Crossbill
Loxia leucoptera
Le Bec-croisé à ailes blanches

You might see mixed flocks of crossbills
and redpolls in the winter, feeding along
roadsides. The crossbills eat the salt that
is put on the roads to melt the snow. The
crossbill is a strange-looking bird with a
lower bill that does not fit directly below
its upper bill, but crosses to one side or the
other. The crossbill uses the tips of its bill
to hold the scales of a conifer cone apart
while the seeds between are removed with
its tongue.

The crossbill's "cheet, cheet" call can be
rather harsh and strident, but when singing
this bird can sometimes sound almost like
a canary trilling; it also produces a variety
of warbles and rattles.

6-6.75", 15-17 cm; 3-4 eggs, pale bluish or
greenish white, spotted with shades of brown or
purple; nest of twigs, lichens, bark shreds, well
out on branch of conifer; sometimes winters
south to central U.S.

22 Common (American) Goldfinch

Spinus tristis

Le Chardonneret jaune

One spring morning I looked out the window of our cottage near Ithaca, New York, and saw an amazing sight: an apple tree there had sprouted scores of lemons overnight. In a second they flew away — I had met a flock of goldfinches for the first time.

This little bright yellow bird is sometimes called a "wild canary." More often it is called the "thistle bird." The goldfinch eats the seeds of the thistle, uses thistle down for the lining of its nests and sometimes builds its nest right in the middle of a patch of thistle — or at least not far from a good supply. The nest is so durable it may last several years.

When the female goldfinch is on the nest, the male often circles overhead. When she is hungry, she cries a sharp, loud "tee-tee-tee" and the male immediately drops to feed her. When she is being fed, she acts just like a nestling: she flutters her wings and gapes like a hungry baby. The male continues to feed both nestlings and the female while she broods the young.

Goldfinches molt in the fall and in winter the male is much like the female, a dull olive-yellow. Before the next breeding season, he will molt again to his brighter plumage.

Listen for the goldfinch's song "perchickaree" and watch for its deeply undulating flight when you see flocks of small birds.

4.5-5.5", 11-14 cm; 4-6 eggs, pale bluish-white, unmarked; winters southern Canada to Gulf of Mexico.

23 Red-eyed Vireo

Vireo olivaceus
Le Viréo aux yeux rouges

The Red-eyed Vireo is a small green bird that is seldom seen but often heard. No other bird sings as persistently as the vireo. It sings all day, pausing only when it catches an insect. This bird is called "preacher" because of its song: a long-continued series of two-to-five note phrases that end with a rising inflection, as a question does. To some it sounds as if the vireo has been giving a long sermon — and then asking if it has been understood.

In spring courtship, the male rocks back and forth with his feathers sleeked back and sings to the female in a whispered voice. After mating, she starts to build a deeply cupped nest, but she often stops halfway through and starts a new nest, using much of the material of the first.

Though the vireo sings constantly in spring and summer, it migrates in silence, one or two mixed in with large flocks of warblers. You can distinguish the vireos because they fly more gracefully — in a less flitting way — than the warblers.

These birds are always in thick foliage of trees where they pick insects from surrounding leaves. Their main enemies are egg-eating birds and mammals, and the parasitic cowbird whose eggs they often incubate and hatch. The larger cowbird hatchlings get most of the food brought to the nest and the vireo hatchlings do not survive.

5.3-6.5", 14-17 cm; 2-4 eggs, white with tiny brown spots; nest suspended from forked, horizontal low branch; winters South America.

24 Black-and-white Warbler

Mniotilta varia
La Fauvette noir et blanc

Look for the pretty little Black-and-white Warbler creeping around on low branches of trees. It hops from branch to branch snatching up insects. It is a fairly common bird and tends to migrate late and return early, making your chances of seeing it even better.

Despite its name, the Black-and-white Warbler doesn't warble but sings a high-pitched, thin "weesee weesee weesee weesee weesee weesee weesee." (Yes, it usually sings "weesee" at least seven times.)

Black-and-white Warblers build their nests on the ground, usually at the base of a tree or a stump, or beside a log or stone. The nest is always well concealed with leaves.

Warblers migrate mainly at night, and when low clouds force them to fly close to the ground they crash into buildings. Lights from these buildings attract and confuse many birds; on overcast nights sometimes thousands are killed.

Most warblers are difficult to identify in the fall because they've molted into similar, drab fall plumages from brightly colored spring feathers. But the Black-and-white Warbler is one with which you'll have no trouble.

4.5-5.5", 10-14 cm; 4-5 eggs, white or creamy white with dots or blotches of shades of brown; winters from Florida to South America.

25 Myrtle Warbler

Dendroica coronata
La Fauvette à croupion jaune

Myrtle Warblers are probably the most
abundant wood warblers in Canada and in
the spruce forests of the northern U.S.
In the north in winter, they eat a great
many bayberries, and — in coastal areas —
the berries of the wax myrtle, thus their
name. Since they digest only the outer
covering of most berries, the seeds that are
eliminated from their bodies can still germi-
nate. They also eat insects, and in the
south in winter drink the juice of fallen
oranges. I've seen them drinking the sweet
sap of sugar maples (and eating the insects
attracted to the sap) and also pecking at
hedge apples.

In spring, during courtship, males fluff their
feathers, raise their wings, erect their crown
feathers, and hop from twig to twig after
females, singing and fluttering all the while.
After mating, they build their deeply cupped
nest, embedding feathers in the lining so
that the tops bend inward over the cup.
The feathers form a screen over the eggs.
The nest is seldom seen, since it sits out on
a branch, high up in a tree. After the young
are hatched, they are fed often by the
parents — about once every eleven minutes.

The song of this bird sounds like the rattle
of a small chain. You can also identify it
by its jerky flight, by the sharp flip of its
tail when it lands, and of course by its
yellow rump and crown.

5-6", 13-15 cm; 4-5 eggs, white, creamy white,
spotted with brown; winters central U.S. to
central Panama.

26 Chestnut-sided Warbler
Dendroica pensylvanica
La Fauvette à flancs marron

If you hear the song "very very pleased to meetcha" near bushes or low plants, look for a bird flitting about with its tail elevated and its wings drooping. Sometimes it hovers like a hummingbird to pick insects off leaves. This is the Chestnut-sided Warbler, one of the prettiest wood warblers.

These birds were once rare in North America. Audubon saw them only once, a flock of five in 1808. But happily their numbers increased greatly after the lands were cleared. The briars and bushes that grow in such places are ideal for these birds.

Their nest is flimsy and loose walled, bound together by insect silk and built low in shrubs or hedgerows.

When an intruder approaches, the male and female react differently. The female drops to the ground and moves slowly, as if injured, away from the nest. But the male flutters from branch to branch, vibrating his wings and spreading his tail to attract the intruder's attention. Both of these responses distract intruders, keeping them from the nest.

The Chestnut-sided Warbler molts in July, so that in the fall the bird is very different in appearance: the chestnut on its sides is greatly reduced, its upper parts are greenish yellow, there is no streaking, and the yellow and black on the head are missing.

4.5-5.3", 11-14 cm; 3-5 eggs, white spotted with browns and grays; winters in Central America.

27 Ovenbird

Seiurus aurocapillus
La Fauvette couronnée

The Ovenbird always builds its nest in a
depression on the ground of deciduous
forests. Leaf litter arching over the nest
gives it the appearance of an old Dutch
oven — thus the bird's name. The Ovenbird
is also called "teacher bird" because it
repeats "cherta-cherta-cherta" five to fif-
teen times, each time louder than the time
before. The vibrating motion of the bird's
tail and body when it walks has given it
other names: "wood-wagtail" and "wagtail
warbler."

Instead of foraging in trees and shrubs as
most warblers do, the Ovenbird leads the
life of a thrush. It walks along the forest
floor scanning the fallen leaves for snails,
insects and spiders.

The female leaves her well-hidden nest
several times a day to feed since, contrary
to other species, male Ovenbirds rarely
feed their females. When she leaves the
nest she walks a great distance before
taking flight. When flushed, she may limp
as far as fifty feet from the nest to draw
the intruder away before flying off.

Many Ovenbirds are killed during migration
by crashing into lighted buildings, TV
towers and airport ceilometers. The way
to prevent this is to turn off as many lights
as possible in tall buildings, especially those
that face north and those that are on for
cosmetic reasons only. Birds face enough
natural dangers when migrating without
our adding man-made ones as well.

5.5-6.5", 14-15 cm, 3-6 eggs, white with reddish
brown and lilac spots that form a wreath around
the large end; winters from Southern U.S. to
Venezuela.

28 Common Yellowthroat
Geothlypis trichas
La Fauvette masquée

With his black mask the male yellowthroat looks somewhat like a bandit. He sings a rhythmical "witchity, witchity, witchity" that to some people sounds like "I beseech you, I beseech you, I beseech you." Yellowthroats have been caught mimicking the songs of marsh wrens and other birds that live in similar habitats. They are readily attracted to squeaking noises made by humans.

Typical warblers, the yellowthroats are constantly on the move gleaning insects from plants. One birdwatcher counted the number of aphids taken by a yellow-throat in one minute — an amazing 89!

Yellowthroats like marshes, thickets and low-growing bushes, and their bulky cup-shaped nests are securely lodged in cattails, briars or even smaller plants like skunk cabbage. But with their low nesting habits, yellowthroats fall victim to a variety of snakes and mammals. In marshes they face added dangers from large fish, turtles and bullfrogs.

Cowbirds often lay their eggs in yellow-throat nests. Sometimes the female yellowthroat builds a second floor to the nest over the top of the cowbird eggs. But usually yellowthroats incubate the cowbird eggs and raise them as their own. Yellowthroats feed their young for a particularly long time. They're still feeding their second brood right up to the time for fall migration, though these young can fly as well as adults and seem perfectly capable of feeding themselves long before then.

If skies are overcast during migration, yellowthroats often crash into buildings and towers and are killed.

4.5-5.7", 10-15 cm; 3-5 eggs, white dotted with gray and shades of brown which form a wreath at large end; winters southern U.S. to Panama, Puerto Rico.

29 American Redstart
Setophaga ruticilla
La Fauvette flamboyante

"Redstart" is an Old English word meaning "red tail." This bird was so named by early settlers because it reminded them of an Old World bird with a red tail.

This brightly colored, commonly seen bird is one of the most active of the little insect-eating wood warblers. Redstarts make lightning-fast dashes after insects. Often their tails and wings are spread to show their bright color as they hop from limb to limb. The redstart's bill is hooked, which helps to deflect insects into its open gape.

The redstart's song is varied, and similar to the Yellow Warbler's, so it takes practice to recognize it. The song has a lispy, short, monotonous "weechy" sound. Males sing from the spring until July.

The female redstart is a precise nest builder. After lining her nest with feathers and hair, she draws in any loose ends from around the cup of the nest and uses them to bind the lining to the frame of the cup. Her brooding drive is very strong. If young hatchlings are removed, she continues to brood the empty nest as if they were still there. On rainy days she spreads her wings over her young and on sunny days she shades them, panting to keep her own body temperature down.

Redstarts spend their winter in Cuba and South America. Cubans call this bird "candelita" (little candle) because it reminds them of a flickering flame as the bird darts from tree to tree.

4.7-5.7", 12-15 cm; 3-5 eggs, white spotted with browns and grays; winters from Mexico to Northern Brazil.

30 Scarlet Tanager

Piranga olivacea
Le Tangar écarlate

Even though the Scarlet Tanager has a loud song and brilliant plumage, it is seldom seen. One reason is that its song resembles that of a robin, but is harsher. People who hear the song often assume it is a robin and don't look further. Also, the Scarlet Tanager lives far away from people — usually in deciduous woods. Even when flying overhead, the tanager might go unnoticed. Without the sun's rays on its plumage, it looks dark rather than brilliant red.

Look among oaks for these tanagers. Their nests are built high in the trees and are so flimsy that you can sometimes see the outline of the eggs through the bottom. Tanagers move slowly, searching for insects high in the trees. Experts at this method of feeding, tanagers miss almost nothing — including the nocturnal moths that are almost impossible for us to detect when they are at rest on leaves and bark during the day. In migration, you might see tanagers at woodland edges or feeding in newly plowed fields along with black-birds. Listen for their call note, "chip-kurr."

In late summer, Scarlet Tanagers that have patches of green feathers mixed in their red plumage might be seen. These are molting males whose plumage will soon be entirely green, much as the females are year round.

After this molt the birds will fly to South America for the winter. Most kinds of tanagers, all beautiful, brightly colored birds, live in the tropics of Central and South America year round.

6.5-7.6", 15-19 cm; 3-5 eggs, pale blue or green, spotted with browns.

31 Cardinal
Richmondena cardinalis
Le Cardinal

Cardinals were originally birds of the South, but since the first Cardinal was seen as far north as Canada in 1896, these birds have been steadily spreading northward.

A seed-eater, the Cardinal has a short, cone-shaped, pointed bill, large jaw muscles, a strong skull and powerful gizzard. It is not a graceful looking bird — its body shape reminds me of a boxer — but its beautiful plumage and pleasant, whistled song make it a bird that everyone loves to see. So popular is the Cardinal that it is the state bird of Illinois, Indiana, Kentucky, North Carolina, Ohio, Virginia and West Virginia.

When Cardinals begin courting, you'll hear the female sing first; then the male repeats her song. She sings again, and if she changes her song slightly the male will repeat it with the changes.

Nests are built in shrubs in towns and cities, along the sides of streams and in old fields. Male Cardinals look after their young as actively as the female. One observer saw a pair of Cardinals feed their young 178 times in a mere six and a half hours!

Cardinals are not highly migratory. Some stay in the same area year round; others may wander several hundred miles. Strange as it may seem, some move north in the fall. Where food is plentiful, they stay and breed in that area the next spring.

If you want to attract Cardinals to your feeder in the winter, put out sunflower seeds, apples, and bread.

7.5-9.3", 19-24 cm; 3-4 eggs, grayish, bluish, greenish white, dotted and spotted with shades of brown, gray, purple.

32 Rose-breasted Grosbeak

Pheucticus ludovicianus
Le Gros-bec à poitrine rose

This bird is so beautiful, and so lovely is its song, that it is captured and sold as a caged bird in Central America where it winters. Fortunately, songbirds are protected in North America and cannot be taken for commercial sale.

Small flocks of red-breasted males return first in spring, then the duller females. Males sing and display with their heads thrown back showing their colorful breast feathers. Other males retreat and a female is attracted as a result of this display.

The male Rose-breasted Grosbeak incubates the eggs almost as much as the female which few other songbirds do. Often he sings as he sits on the eggs. He also helps to brood the young after the eggs are hatched. (Brooding is essentially sitting on the nestlings, helping to keep their body temperature regulated until their own bodies are capable of temperature control.) He helps the female build the nest and keep it clean, and he teaches the fledglings how to open seeds. Sometimes — after days of teaching — he becomes impatient, pecks them on the head and chases them away.

Look for this bird in bushes and shrubs and among stands of small trees. Listen for a song like the robin's but with shorter pauses between each song. (The robin's pauses are about the length of the song itself; the Rose-breasted Grosbeak pauses only briefly before singing again.)

7-8.5", 18-22 cm; 3-6 eggs, pale gray, blue to green, spotted with brown and purple, wreathed or capped at the large end; flimsy twig nest in fork of small tree or shrub.

33 Indigo Bunting

Passerina cyanea
Le Bruant indigo

Although each is recognizable as the song
of an Indigo Bunting, every male's song
sounds slightly different. The song is loud
at first, then becomes fainter and harsher.
In the spring, males constantly sing from
high open perches until their song sounds
gravelly — presumably when their lungs
begin to give out. They have a call note,
a sharp "chipping" sound, that may be
easier to recognize — it is similar to the
sound of two pebbles being struck together.

The male Indigo Bunting is very aggressive
in defending his territory; thus, he's often
seen while his paler mate stays low in
thickets. Even when you are some distance
from her nest, the female Indigo Bunting
becomes so disturbed that she gives alarm
calls and twitches her tail from side to side.
If the nest is touched when eggs are in it,
the buntings will abandon it, but if the
eggs have hatched, they won't abandon
the nestlings.

If you see an Indigo Bunting smoothing
its beautiful feather coat with its bill, it
may be preening or it may be "anting."
Like some other birds, the Indigo Bunting
spreads the juices of ants on its feathers —
no one knows just why. The deep blue
male Indigo Buntings look like their paler
brown mates in fall and winter.

Watch for these birds in orchards and
wooded roadsides where they feed on
insects. They frequent raspberry and
elderberry bushes when berries are ripe,
and in late summer they can be seen in
cornfields where they find food among
the silks of ripened corn.

5.25-5.75", 13-20 cm; 3-4 eggs, white or pale
bluish white, unmarked; well-woven nest in
crotch of shrub, low tree or bush; winters Cuba,
Central America.

34 Savannah Sparrow
Passerculus sandwichensis
Le Pinson des prés

It may surprise some readers to know that there are many kinds of sparrows. Most have a similar, rather dull, streaked plumage (often with yellow spots) and all have cone-shaped bills. The commonest sparrow in many places, the Savannah Sparrow, can be found in hayfields and meadows, among sand dunes and around marshes from the Arctic to the Tropics. Though a bird of savannahs, it was named not for its habitat but for the city of Savannah, Georgia.

Savannah Sparrows hop along the ground foraging mainly for seeds but, in nesting season, insects and small crustaceans, too. When disturbed, they crouch low with their heads down, and run along the ground rather than fly. When they do fly, it is usually low and for short distances.

This bird's song is a high-pitched buzz, much like an insect might give. It rarely sings in migration, though there is a faint call note — "tseep" — given as it takes off, and repeated while flying.

Those of you who know the Savannah Sparrow may think that the bird illustrated here is too light in color. In fact, it is an "Ipswich Sparrow," a member of an isolated population of the Savannah Sparrow. This bird breeds on one small sand bar of Sable Island 90 miles off the coast of Nova Scotia, and winters along a narrow coastal strip between Nova Scotia and Georgia. There are only two or three thousand of these birds. As the seaside cottages on its wintering range increase, loss of nesting and wintering grounds are future threats to the existence of these birds.

Savannah Sparrow: 5-5.8", 13-15 cm.
Ipswich Sparrow: 5.9-6.5", 15-17 cm.

4-6 eggs, pale greenish blue, blotched with browns; well-concealed nest in hollow or ground.

35 Slate-colored (Dark-eyed) Junco
Junco hyemalis

Le Junco ardoisé

Slate-colored Juncos are sometimes called "snowbirds": you often see flocks of them scratching through snow cover on the ground to find seeds. The junco is one of the most distinctive of the sparrows, not streaked and dull brown like its relatives.

Juncos emit a simple trill, and sometimes sing two to three trills on different pitches to produce a single song. After they've formed pairs, and for the rest of the year, you'll hear them giving a variety of call notes — different ones are given when alarmed, when scolding, when fighting or feeding.

During most of the year, juncos hop along scratching the ground for weed seeds, but, like most songbirds, they feed their nestlings insects. They eat insects themselves at nesting time and in late winter when the early hatching insects have emerged.

In mid-October they start moving south in loose flocks with the birds behaving individually, not flying together as a unit. And in winter, they gather into separate foraging flocks each with its own foraging "territory."

Look for the "snowbird" whether there's snow or not. In fall and winter, throw grain out on the ground in your yard or in a nearby park to attract these pretty little birds.

5.75-6.5", 15-17 cm; 4-5 eggs, pale bluish white, spotted with brown, purple, gray; nest on ground under weeds, grass, fallen tree; winters southern Canada to Gulf of Mexico.

36 White-throated Sparrow
Zonotrichia albicollis
Le Pinson à gorge blanche

New Englanders say the White-throated Sparrow sings "Old Sam Peabody, Peabody, Peabody," but Canadians claim that it sounds more like "Oh sweet Canada, Canada, Canada." Because of its distinctive whistled song, this bird is also known as the "Canadian Song Sparrow," "Poor Sam Peabody" and "Whistle Bird."

It is a common bird, easy to recognize because of the white patch on its throat. If you can't see the patch, you can identify the bird by its behavior. It is the sparrow that scuffles the ground with outspread legs. After scratching the ground this way, it jumps back, throwing the dirt behind it. People have seen White-throated Sparrows scratching for seeds and insects like this for as long as an hour at a time.

Some of these birds have white streaks on their heads and others tan. The white-streaked birds — both male and female — are aggressive, while the tan streaked are not. When these birds mate it is always with birds of different-color streaking. Perhaps if two tan-streaked birds mated, they would not be able to defend their territory; or if two white-streaked birds mated, they would be too aggressive to raise their young. Nesting is more often successful when the unlike pairs of birds mate.

If you see a White-throated Sparrow, watch for others, as it will usually be one of a small flock.

6.3-7.2", 16-18 cm; 3-5 eggs, grayish, bluish, or greenish white, blotched with shades of brown; cup-shaped nest on ground under shrub or clump of grass; winters north-central U.S. to Gulf of Mexico.

37 Song Sparrow
Melospiza melodia
Le Pinson chanteur

Listen for the Song Sparrow on a cold, clear morning in late winter. It begins early, singing as many as six to eight songs per minute and continues all day, though singing with less frequency as the day goes on. To many people, the Song Sparrow signals the beginning of spring. It sings throughout the year but much more frequently and vigorously as spring approaches.

This bird is found almost everywhere in North America: near human dwellings, along river banks and brushy shores of ponds, in wet meadows and along bushy fence rows. You can recognize it by the blackish or brownish spot on its breast or by its actions: look for a sparrow that flies only short distances, from perch to perch, its tail flopping to one side as it flits about in search of food. It also bathes a lot, so watch for it in pools of standing water. It sometimes hits at foliage with its wings and body to knock drops of water onto its plumage.

Song Sparrows sing songs of two general types, but they learn their particular phrasing by listening to other Song Sparrows in the vicinity. Thus a Song Sparrow in Montreal would sound pretty much like one in Quebec City, whereas those from St. Louis or Cincinnati would sing a different tune. But all of these tunes would be recognized as the rich song of the Song Sparrow, a bird welcomed not only for its song, but also because it eats millions of weed seeds and insects.

6-7", 16-18 cm; 3-5 eggs, pale bluish to grayish green speckled with shades of brown; nest on ground or in bush or small tree; winters southern Canada to Gulf of Mexico.

38 Bobolink
Dolichonyx oryzivorus
Le Goglu

Bobolinks have a habit of stopping to eat and roost in the rice fields of the southern United States on their way to and from South America, where they winter. Huge numbers of Bobolinks — or "rice birds" as they are called — were shot by farmers because of the destruction they caused to crops. And because they were considered a restaurant delicacy, plump from the rice on which they fed, many more were shot for the table.

These birds are now protected by law as songbirds, but their numbers are vastly reduced from the time in the 1800's when Bobolinks were seen hovering over the buttercups, daisies and waving grasses in every meadow. Now they're found farther west where hayfields are more plentiful.

In contrast to the gaudy males, female Bobolinks are well camouflaged in the grasses, and stay low in them while nesting. Bobolinks make it practically impossible for an intruder to find their nest. They hop or run along the ground for a great distance from the nest before flying and when they land, it is far from the nest. Then they run back to it.

Male Bobolinks were once captured and sold as singing birds. Their rich song is a loud, clear series of short notes that begin on a low pitch rising higher as the song continues. Males display their plumage and gurgle their songs for females; perhaps no other bird sings so spectacularly in courtship. Their only singing after breeding season is a distinctive "clink" note they make as they fly at night when they migrate in August to the marshy areas of Argentina and Brazil.

6.5-8", 17-20 cm; 4-7 eggs, pale gray or pale brown spotted with shades of brown; nest in hollow on ground in meadows.

39 Eastern Meadowlark

Sturnella magna
La Sturnelle des prés

Farmers in southern Canada and the northern United States welcome the Eastern Meadowlark, the best known of the grassland and woodland birds. It has been estimated that in ten days ten nestlings are fed 5000-7000 grasshoppers by their parents. The parents, too, eat large quantities of destructive insects and noxious weed seeds. But farmers further south consider this bird a pest, as large migrating flocks do considerable damage to crops.

The female meadowlark builds her nest on the ground, in a hoofprint or other depression. She remodels the spot with her sharp, pointed bill and puts surrounding grasses over it. Eventually she builds a dome-shaped roof over the nest. However, about eight days after the nestlings hatch, they become so active that they completely destroy the nest. With no roof over their heads they are exposed to the sun's rays and have to pant vigorously to keep their body temperature from soaring. Sometimes they leave the nest, returning only to be fed.

Meadowlarks sing a plaintive, pleasant-sounding song of whistled notes that sounds like "spring-o-the-yeeeear." They don't sing while incubating their eggs or while molting, but otherwise you can hear meadowlarks at any time of year.

In the Midwest — Kansas, Wisconsin, Manitoba — you are likely to see a bird that looks and acts exactly like the Eastern Meadowlark but sounds quite different. What you are seeing is a Western Meadowlark. In some areas, these two can really confuse you — they occur in the same fields and meadows.

8.5-11", 22-28 cm; 3-7 eggs, white, greatly spotted with lavender and shades of brown; winters rarely southern Ontario to southern U.S.

40 Red-winged Blackbird
Agelaius phoeniceus
Le Carouge à épaulettes

This beautiful bird of marshes and roadside ditches — anywhere there's standing water — is one of the most commonly seen of the eastern birds. Males return from their winter home early in spring, sometimes when the water in marshes is still ice covered, to establish their territories. Females and young males join them in April. The females keep low in the cattails; if they move higher in the vegetation or try to fly, males chase them back.

In early spring, red-wings call softly, and only the yellow margin of their colorful wing patch shows. Later in spring, they display the brilliant red patch on their wings and sing a song that sounds like "konk-la-reeee."

Even in a marsh that has a dense colony of red-wings, each male has its own terri-tory. Females are aggressive toward other females; each selects a nesting territory within an area already established by a male. There are often more females in a marsh than males so polygamy is fairly common. When an intruder approaches the marsh, the male red-wing will circle round the nests of all his mates giving equal protection to all.

Red-winged Blackbirds are beneficial to people while on their breeding grounds because of all the insects they eat. But in migration large flocks do considerable damage to corn and rice crops. Like the Bobolinks, they were once considered table delicacies as "reed" or "rice birds."

7.5-10", 19-25 cm; 3-5 eggs, pale bluish green, spotted or streaked with shades of brown and purple; loosely woven nest in cattails, sedges etc., near water; winters southern U.S.

41 Baltimore (Northern) Oriole
Icterus galbula
L'Oriole de Baltimore

Baltimore Orioles are like spring flowers: they arrive suddenly and in great splendor, then disappear too soon. (In fact, they don't leave until the fall, but after their flurry of nest building they become so inconspicuous that you rarely notice them.)

If you see a long, hanging nest suspended high in a tree, you'll know it was made by a Baltimore Oriole. Since they often come back to a site year after year, watch the same place for nest building the following year. While the female is building, the male displays his plumage and sings a loud warble interspersed with chattering notes. A day or two before the young are ready to leave the nest, you might see nestlings clinging to the outside, crawling in and out. After nesting season, the young birds and females form feeding flocks; adult males remain alone until migration.

Orioles eat huge quantities of caterpillars, even haired and spiny ones that most birds avoid. They also eat other insects and spiders and some wild fruits. Unfortunately, they like cultivated peas and small fruits and can damage crops in areas where flocks are large. More delicate eaters than the robin, they don't gulp whole cherries and grapes but pierce the skin with their beaks and sip the juice.

Baltimore Orioles spread westward with settlers, taking advantage of the clumps of willows and poplars that were planted as shade trees.

This pretty bird was named for British colonist, Lord Baltimore, whose family colors were orange and black.

7-8.2", 17-20 cm; 4-6 eggs, pale grayish white, streaked or blotched with browns and black; winters Central America.

42 Common Grackle (Bronzed, Purple Grackle)

Quiscalus quiscula
Le Mainate bronzé

This beautiful, shiny blackbird — whose metallic colors change with the angle of the sun — is common in backyards and city parks. The noisy and aggressive grackle, sometimes called "crow black-bird," is similar to the crow in many ways, although the crow is larger and stockier, and not closely related.

The male's hoarse, grating song has been described as sounding like the squeak of a rusty hinge. Other people have been even less kind in their descriptions. But female grackles respond to it and soon nests are being built in shade trees and orchards.

The grackle is the goat of the bird world: it will eat almost anything. It nest robs, like the Blue Jay, eating eggs and killing the young. It frequents areas where gar-bage is available. Grackles have been seen wading body deep in water and even plunging in from overhanging tree roots. There they catch insects and snails, and dig crayfish from under stones. Holding the crayfish in their bills, they hammer it against rocks to open it. Grackles have also been seen seizing goldfish from small pools and frogs from ponds. They eat seeds, and take in sand or gravel to help grind the seeds.

Grackles migrate in huge numbers, even into the millions. Observers have seen flocks which are a quarter of a mile in width and which take more than an hour to pass overhead.

11-13.5", 28-34 cm; 4-6 eggs, pale greenish white, blotched with dark browns, purples; loose bulky nests, usually in small colonies; winters mainly southern U.S.

43 Brown-headed Cowbird

Molothrus ater
Le Vacher à tête brune

The cowbird's Greek name — "Molothrus" — means vagabond or parasite, and it is apt for this is the only parasitic songbird in the east. The female cowbird makes no nest; instead she lays her eggs in the nests of other birds throwing out one of the host bird's eggs to make room for her own.

Birds respond to this new egg in a variety of ways: some desert the nest, some build a new floor over the cowbird egg, some throw the egg out, and others accept the egg and raise the young cowbird as their own. Cowbird hatchlings grow quickly, and I have often seen the rather sad and ridiculous sight of a tiny warbler being followed by a cowbird two to three times its size, gaping to be fed.

Cowbirds have been seen feeding young cowbirds in the nests of other birds. (It is not known if the bird doing the feeding is the same one that.laid the egg.) The cowbird won't feed the other hatchlings in the nest and even pecks at them if they try to take food from her.

Cowbirds search the grass for insects that are stirred by grazing cattle. This habit gives them their name; they were earlier known as "buffalo birds." They often forage along roadsides for insects that have been stunned by passing cars. Watch for a bird that walks or runs, seldom hopping, with its tail held high and with its wings drooping. It sings squeaking, shrill notes.

7-8.25", 18-21 cm; 6 eggs, white or grayish white dotted with shades of brown; usually in different nests, sometimes more than one egg per nest; after 3 or 4 days a second clutch laid (3 or 4 clutches per season); winters southern Ontario to southern Mexico.

White-breasted Nuthatch
Sitta carolinensis
La Sittelle à poitrine blanche

Some nuthatches stick soft-shelled nuts —
such as acorns, pine nuts, and chestnuts —
into crevices in bark and peck away at
them to crack the shells, thus their name.

Nuthatches move not up but down a tree —
headfirst — and around limbs, constantly
on the watch for insects. The nuthatch
climbs downward by anchoring itself with
its upper foot. With one toe forward and
three back, just the opposite of most
perching birds, it hangs securely while it
peers into crevices below for insects. The
nuthatch and many other birds that search
for insects in crevices have white breasts
which reflect light, perhaps making it
easier for the bird to see inside.

The best way to find nuthatches (and Brown
Creepers) is to listen for the easily recognized song of the chickadee. These birds
are often found searching in the same
woodland for insect food. You'll hear the
nasal "yank" of the nuthatches all year
round. Attract them to your feeder with
sunflower seeds and suet. (See illustration
No. 14.)

5.2-6.2", 13-16 cm; 5-9 eggs, white, spotted with
light brown; nest of bark shreds, twigs, fur, in
cavities in trees or nest boxes.